RETIREMENT
SIMPLIFIED

The Simple Two-Step Formula to
Retire Wealthy & Worry-Free

DANIEL RONDBERG

CASS AND SPENCE PUBLISHING

Published by Cass & Spence Publishing LLC, Arizona
Disclaimer

This publication is designed to provide accurate and authoritative information about the subject matter covered. It is sold to understand that the publisher is not engaged in rendering legal, accounting, or other professional advice. If legal advice or further expert assistance is required, a competent professional's services should be sought.

The author wishes to acknowledge the respective sources for the use of graphs, charts, and other data in this book. The author intends to portray that data accurately rather than through representations.
This book may contain technical or other errors. Daniel Rondberg and The Rondberg Companies do not guarantee its accuracy, completeness, or suitability. In no event shall Daniel Rondberg or The Rondberg Companies be liable for any special, indirect, or consequential damages relating to this material for any use of this material or any referenced website and courses or the application of any idea or strategy in this book.

Daniel Rondberg and The Rondberg Companies provide the information in this book, and it is offered for educational

Dedication

To my Dad, who dedicated his life to
always being there for me.

He taught me how to be the man, husband,
and father that I am proud to be.

This is for you!

Table of Contents

My Story

Have you ever read a book to learn how to do something? Did you wish the author would get right to the point so that you could obtain the knowledge you need and start using it right away? Was the book filled with fluff that tried to prove to you how smart the author is? Were you frustrated sifting through unnecessary pages? Have you ever finished reading a book and realized the information you actually wanted to know could have been explained in 50 pages instead of 200 pages? Me, too!

So, enter my new career as an Amazon Short Reads author. I will be writing a series of short books that will, in less than 100 pages, deliver the best strategies I have gained in my career as a retirement consultant. My day job is to help clients create security and certainty in their retirement. I love what I do – so much that I pride myself on providing as much value as I can to each client. My passion is sharing the non-conventional, most valuable, and meaningful information that can make a tremendous difference in others' lives.

In 2018, I realized that I could only help so many people through one-on-one meetings. So, I accepted an offer to travel the country, bringing my message to the financial community.

I was hired to speak to and train insurance agents, financial advisors, CPAs, and attorneys on strategies for retirees to maximize the Tax Cuts and Jobs Act (The Tax Reform). My theory was that if I spoke to 100 financial professionals at once, and each had 100 clients, I was significantly expanding my impact and potentially helping many more people.

Introduction

I wrote *Retirement Simplified* for the same woman I meet at the end of all my live workshops. I've met her many times over the years. She is usually in her 70's. She is a kind and sweet woman. I imagine her sneaking cookies and treats to her grandkids. She finds her way to me at the end of every class and says something like this:

> *"That was really great information, but I'm not sure if you can help me. I live on my Social Security check, and I had to move in with my daughter. My husband passed, I no longer receive his Social Security check, and his pension payments have stopped. We canceled our life insurance policy, and I have no money."*

I have spent so much time with these women who are desperate to find a solution that isn't there. Being a husband and a father of two girls, I never want any of the women in my family to echo these words as a result of my decisions. Now, let me pause. I do not believe that we are stuck in the 1940's, where only the men work, and the women live and die by their husband's ability to earn and save money. Women are strong, smart, and independent and making more money than men now. This is not a wage equality issue. It is a life expectancy issue—women typically outlive men.

In fact, for every widower we have as a client, we have nine widows. Ultimately, it's the woman who will realize the consequences of the financial decisions she and her spouse made during their life together.

I do not want to leave anyone out. This book is equally essential for that single man. He faces as much risk as do the women that attend my workshops.

After helping hundreds of people and speaking to thousands more, I know there is only one thing that separates women who retire with money and those who retire with no money: how well they executed the two-step formula that I'm about to share with you. *Retirement Simplified* is part of the **No Stone Left Unturned** series dedicated to educating others on achieving financial freedom.

Personal finance isn't taught in schools. Most of us learn it from our parents. Their financial habits, good or bad, usually help us determine how we want our lives to go.

Money and finances are the leading cause of divorce in the United States. It's not uncommon for people to incur tremendous stress and endure subsequent health problems from the lack of means for proper medical care or to be able to provide adequate nutrition.

Money can do many things:

- Dictate your expressions of love for your spouse, family, and friends.
- Dictate our free time.
- Make us do things we hate for years.
- Cause depression and anxiety.
- Cause us to be people that we are not.
- Cause us to cross moral agreements and break laws.
- Drive us away from people.
- Make us bitten, envious, miserable.
- Take away from us experiencing this world to the fullest with the one life we get.

Money can also:

- Provide freedom in our lives.
- Allow us to live like kings and queens compared to the rest of the world.
- Allow us to give back and share love and joy with others who need help.
- Provide the most amazing experiences. We can travel the world with our family and friends, sampling and enjoying all of the culture and natural wonder our souls can handle.
- Provide us time to enjoy life and pursue the passions we truly want.
- Provide you everything you need to live your life to the fullest.
- Be a legacy that allows your family to take control and break the cycle of poverty.

▢ Be an afterthought. A tool. A means to living the life you've always wanted.

No Stone Left Unturned

When my wife and I had our first daughter, everything in my life changed. My priorities and desires changed. I was obsessed with only one thing: spending time with my wife and daughter. I had a great career, but unless I was there to work, I had no income. It hurt knowing that I was trapped. I grew miserable trying to comprehend that I had to leave this little girl and the love of my life every morning and be apart from them all day. I had no choice.

I sought out people, education, and tools that promised the highest income possible. I spent tens of thousands of dollars investing in products to learn how to make or save money. It began to consume me, and every conversation with a peer in the financial industry became about my quest. With a successful career that began at J.P. Morgan and moved to a specialization in helping people mitigate retirement risks, I had an excellent background in all of the traditional financial education.

I began to search for methods that weren't conventional but that successful entrepreneurs were using with great results. I adopted a *No Stone Left Unturned* approach. I formed masterminds, conducted interviews, and collected knowledge and experience like an addiction. I traveled the country to speak and meet people and bought every book and course I could find. When my clients went to see their CPAs and attorneys, I went with them. I volunteered to help write the offering memorandum for a hedge fund, joined financial associations, and stayed up all night many times studying for licensing exams. I got a second job in the mortgage business and attended symposiums and lectures all over the country. I looked under as many stones as I could and still do. I am an eternal student of finance. So, I decided to package my experience and knowledge and share it in a series I call *No Stone Left Unturned*.

My first book, "No Stone Left Unturned," shares how I was hired in 2018 to travel the country to speak to financial professionals. This book and every book after is part of the *No Stone Left Unturned* series, which shares the most powerful concepts that I've learned and now use in my own life to help you achieve financial freedom and retire successfully. My message is designed to be explained in less than 100 pages to get the information you need quickly and turn around and apply the concepts to your life.

After speaking to financial professionals and working in their practices, I realized there is a large gap in financial knowledge in our country. It is the difference between living the life you want and struggling to make choices that aren't centered around your paycheck.

I also discovered that most of the financial education we do get has the intent to sell us something. Either that or it's so boring and overly complicated that it does not engage us and, therefore, is useless. No one ever changed their life by reading half of a book and moving on. However, when people embrace a new idea that they understand and align it with their actions, significant changes can occur and inspire them to take action to transform their lives for the better. I have made it my mission to deliver this information effectively so you can retire from the life you don't want and start living the life you do want.

Thank you for reading.

The Simple Two-Step Retirement Formula

So, you're thinking about retirement? Are you all set? Have you met with your financial planner? Did you map out your income, discuss all your hopes and dreams, and learn how to structure your income to match the realization of those visions? Did you work your entire life and save as much as possible in a 401(k)? Did you do everything that Dave Ramsey told you to do? Suze Orman? Tony Robbins?

How about Tom Hegna?

Most people have heard the first three names, but not enough people are familiar with that last one. Dave Ramsey, Suze Orman, and Tony Robbins have emerged as some of the most well-respected and biggest names in personal finance, but Tom...? Tom is special. He's not a household name, but Tom is as prominent and well-respected as they come in the retirement business world. Why? Because Tom gets credit for the Two-Step Retirement Formula that is proven and works every single time. Before you panic and think, "Oh my goodness, another format, I already studied, planned, confirmed, and prepared."

Don't worry. Tom's formula is probably the simplest there is to ensure you have success in retirement. As an economist, his isn't the first book on the shelf at Barnes and Noble, his program isn't taught in small church groups, and he doesn't have 10 million YouTube subscribers.

But Tom travels the globe and speaks directly to the largest financial institutions worldwide. Name any company, and chances are Tom has spoken with their executives, top analysts, actuaries, and retail advisors. He focuses only on retirement. He has written five books, worked as a Fortune 500 Vice President, and is the number one authority on retirement in the world. Tom is the person you need when it's retirement time. His book, "Don't Worry, Retire Happy," and his white paper, "Retirement Alpha," are arguably the two most significant publications for people retiring in the next ten years.

In 2020, the COVID-19 pandemic caused massive unemployment, foreclosures, bailouts, interest rate reductions, market volatility, and general uncertainty. If you were directly affected by this, Tom's Two-Step formula is your way of taking back your life and ensuring you get the happily-ever-after you have worked your entire life to achieve.

This book will break down the contents of these two publications and share my process to execute this formula. Before we get started, I want you to take a deep breath. Thinking about retirement can be stressful, and having worked helping people with retirement for almost ten years, I understand that. My goal is to give you every tactic our business employs to allow our clients to retire successfully and happily. After reading this book, I want you to feel confident, informed, and excited about your retirement.

I aim to deliver this information in an entertaining manner to keep you engaged. Buckle up and prepare to learn the retirement formula that works in any economy.

What is the Simple Two-Step Formula for Retirement?

Step One: Cover all your basic needs and expenses with *Guaranteed Lifetime Income.*

Step Two: Remove all other retirement risks.

Wow, that *is* simple, right? Tom says it becomes simpler and simpler the longer he studies it, and he has been studying retirement for more than 30 years. But what does it mean, and how can it be so simple?

There are many retirement philosophies, such as the four percent rule, the two percent rule, the perennial income approach, FIRE, and on and on. While I won't waste time explaining each of these approaches, I will say this: Retirement is about one thing—**Income**. Retired people need their income to last longer than they do.

Each year, AARP surveys its members and asks seniors, "What is your number one fear?

Can you guess the most common answer? Hint: it's NOT dying.

If you guessed, "Outliving my money," you just won access to my free course, "Are You SURE You're Ready to Retire?"

We currently have a retirement crisis putting a huge question mark after your happily-ever-after because, in the late eighties and early nineties, 90 percent of the corporations in America began to eliminate the time-honored pension. Until then, companies rewarded employees for their years of dedication, hard work, and loyalty. However, corporations discovered it was much less expensive to set up 401(k) programs and match a percentage of employee contributions than to provide a guaranteed income through a company pension for the rest of the employee's and their spouse's lives.

It's no surprise that left to their own devices, 50 percent of Americans save less than $25,000 for retirement, and 45 percent of Americans save nothing. I could write an entire book about the retirement crisis and America's 401(k)s. If you like your 401(k), TSP, 403(b), SEP, Deferred Comp, great. I don't blame these companies or their employer-sponsored profit-sharing plans for the situation. I'm saying that it's human nature to live in the moment.

Unfortunately, most people don't consider that we now live longer than humans at any other time in history. The population of centenarians is the fastest growing population on the planet. We know more about medicine and nutrition than ever before. As Tom put it, all other philosophies are suboptimal compared to Guaranteed Income because,

---

"It is impossible to optimize the withdrawal of your assets over the indefinite period of a human life."

Let me say this another way. If you knew that you would die tomorrow, you could really let loose today and live it up. If you live to be 105 years old, you must ask yourself if the money you saved can provide you with a paycheck for all those years. You must think of retirement as being out of work for 40 years. It's no longer earn and *save*; it's now *withdraw and spend*. For how long? No one knows.

Because you don't know, it is virtually impossible to ensure your retirement strategy is set up to withdraw the most efficient amount at just the right time. Enter **Step One of the Simple Two-Step Retirement Formula**. Cover all your basic needs and expenses with *Guaranteed Lifetime Income.*

Part One:
Guaranteed Life Income

Step One:
Guaranteed Lifetime Income

Step One of the Simple Two-Step Retirement Formula is to cover all your basic needs and expenses with *Guaranteed Lifetime Income*. Let's talk about what that is and why it is the first step.

Guaranteed Lifetime Income comes in three forms: Social Security, Pensions, and Annuities.

I'm going to stop here for a second. You might be thinking, *I have heard annuities are bad. Right?* If you have been reading my work for a while, you know that I do not call a financial instrument good or bad. I also strongly encourage my readers to open their thinking and avoid attaching personal opinions and emotions, or worse, market manipulations on financial products and their purposes.

Each product is a unique tool that does a specific job. If you use the wrong tool for a job, you'll most likely get poor results. Using the right tool for the right job at the right time and the chances increase that you will achieve the desired result.

Social Security, Annuities, and Pensions

Social Security is America's favorite annuity. Pensions are YOUR favorite annuity. I hear all the time, "Oh, I just missed the cut-off to be lucky enough to earn a pension. Annuities are bad, right?"

Social Security and pensions provide a guaranteed paycheck for the rest of your life. An annuity, at its core, guarantees lifetime income; in other words, an annuity provides a guaranteed paycheck for the rest of your life. So, when people tell me annuities are bad, I ask, "Why do you think that?" I don't ask to be a wise guy. I genuinely ask them to understand their experience, current knowledge on the topic, and belief systems that shape how they will make financial decisions and embrace financial solutions. Ninety percent of the time, they respond with, "I've just heard that."

OK, fair enough. Someone somewhere said annuities were bad. Is it true? Rather than a fact, it's an opinion. Actually, it's more than an opinion; it's a dedicated marketing strategy used by financial professionals who pay millions of dollars for ads because it's incredibly highly effective, and they are compensated using a fee-based model. The marketing strategy says annuities are bad, so allow me to show you the "good" solution that I can offer (sell to) you. It works for these marketers, and that's why they pay millions for it.

If you buy an annuity for Guaranteed Lifetime Income, the likelihood of the financial professional who sold it to you taking control of your account and managing it on your behalf in exchange for a lifetime of collecting fees is very low.

Annuities: Are they good or bad? I compare it as me trying to convince you that a hammer is bad. That's ridiculous. An annuity is what it is, a tool.

Beethoven, Babe Ruth, and Ben Bernanke are among other famous people who have used annuities to create retirement security. The German government paid Beethoven with annuities to free his mind from the burden of finances, allowing him to compose at his best freely. Can you imagine? If you had an endless guaranteed cash flow that was more than you needed every single month, what things in your life would you be free to truly enjoy to the fullest? Those things, your dreams, are possible when using annuities.

See Beethoven's annuity agreement below.

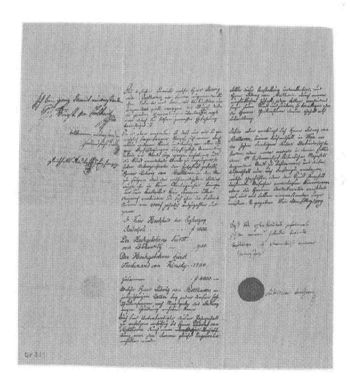

Longevity Risk in Retirement (Outliving Your Money)

A 2018 Guaranteed Lifetime Income Study conducted by Greenwald & Associates and CANNEX gathered information from 1,003 individuals between the ages of 55 and 75 and whose household assets were at least $100,000. Respondents said the greatest benefits of having a protected lifetime income are protections against longevity risk, peace of mind, and being better able to budget – all of which can make for a less stressful and happier overall retirement.

Think about a senior you know that has been collecting a pension for many years. You may have noticed they don't worry about money because they get a check every month. If they spend it all one month on something fun or even medical expenses, guess what? They aren't panicked because another check will arrive next month.

When you retire with assets and only your Social Security check, you encounter one of the first retirement challenges. How much can you withdraw to fill that gap between Social Security and what you need to pay your bills? How can you do it, so you don't run out of money? Great questions. Have you ever heard the phrase, "buy and hold?" It always works. Always. There is never a time in the history of our economy that this hasn't worked.

But there's a reason it doesn't work in retirement. Because it's no longer about "buy and hold"; instead, it is now "hold and distribute." Your mortgage and groceries do not care what your stock prices are that month when money is needed to fill those needs. You will need money and will sell in both highs and lows. Even when the market dips, you will need to take out more and more money. As you diminish those investments, you have less money to help you recover when the market goes up again.

Sequence of Withdrawals Risk

The sequence and timing of withdrawals from a retirement account can **damage the investor's overall return**. Account withdrawals during a bear market are costlier than the same withdrawals in a bull market. A diversified portfolio is the best protection for your savings against sequence risk. Years ago, you could walk into any bank in America and get a six percent CD, and then you could live off the interest earned and never touch the principal. Since interest rates have been at historic lows for more than a decade, you can no longer do this. Enter interest rate risk and my segue into Part 2, where I will explain this and other retirement risks in further detail.

The Two-Step formula works because if you cover all your needs with Guaranteed Lifetime Income, you cannot run out of money. Then, if you remove the risks to that income, your probability of success grows to nearly 100 percent. Short of developing a gambling addiction, it is almost foolproof.

Risk is the possibility of something going wrong. If Murphy's law has taught us anything, it's what can go wrong will go wrong. If you leave risk on the table, you're increasing the probability that something will go wrong. These risks to your retirement income could damage your standard of living if not addressed. People never run out of money, thanks to Social Security. However, they can and do decrease their standard of living. If you have ever been through this with a family member, you know that it's stressful for everyone involved. It's uncomfortable, and it ultimately strips the senior of his or her dignity and independence. None of us envision this scenario for our happily ever after.

So, what is a safe withdrawal rate from a diversified portfolio? What percentage can you withdraw confidently without running out of money? It used to be four percent, but according to Morning Star, now it is two percent. So if you have $1,000,000, Congratulations! You can withdraw $20,000 per year to live on and feel confident that you will not run out of money. Why is this figure so low? Because people today live longer, interest rates are extremely low, and there has been significant volatility in the market. What do you do now? Keep reading to learn more.

Bonus Strategy —
Increasing Withdrawal Rates from Your Portfolio

Let's say a couple has $1,000,000 in retirement savings in a 401(k), are five years away from retiring, and need the money now. Their portfolio also has a "target fund" with a 60/40 portfolio, which means 60 percent is at risk, and 40 percent is safe.

The couple receives Social Security but also needs another $2,500 from that 401(k) each month to cover all expenses. A monthly $2,500 withdrawal is $30,000 annually, which is three percent of the $1,000,000 in savings. With retirement five years away, there is a relatively short horizon until they will need their money. Five years is not enough time to withstand a market correction and wait for recovery. What do they do?

With the aim of a successful retirement, they can't sustain too much risk during the next five years. If they replace only the safe portion of their 401(k) or the 40 percent that pays them less than two percent with a deferred income annuity, in five years, that $400,000 annuity will provide them the $2,500 they need monthly. This way, achieving their goal is assured! No longer do they have to try to use the entire portfolio to generate the income. Instead, they only need $400,000 of it. They are free to pursue a more efficient strategy utilizing their own money rather than trying to leave 40 percent on the sidelines to stay safe. Over time, the overall returns almost always increase.

In his book, "Retirement Alpha," Tom Hegna lays all of this out. The $2,500 monthly amount equals a 13.33 percent payout rate of the original $400,000. Instead of dedicating $1,000,000 to generate the $30,000 needed, you can guarantee that only 40 percent or $400,000 will be dedicated to the job. This tactic guarantees the highest routine income for the least amount of money. In effect, you remove longevity risk, sequence risk, and the order of returns risk. We'll talk more about those retirement risks in Part Two.

Any reference to an insurance policy guaranty is referencing the contractual guarantees. This is general insurance information, is not a specific recommendation, and should not be applied to anyone's individual situation. I am not a CPA, Attorney, or Advisor; speak with your team of advisors and council. I am not endorsing or discussing any specific product or any one company.

I am also not making any guaranty that these strategies will work for you. Guarantees rely on the financial strength and claims-paying ability of the issuing insurer. Any application must be completed by a qualified licensed professional that you decide to work with. Not all products are available in all states. Surrender charges may apply to the surrender charge period. These products are not guaranteed by any bank or credit union and are not issued by the FDIC or any other federal government agency.

Key Takeaways

- What is the biggest fear among seniors? Outliving their money.
- The greatest benefits of having a protected lifetime income are protections against longevity risk, peace of mind, and being better able to budget – all of which can make for a less stressful and happier overall retirement.

Part Two:
Key Retirement Risks

Step Two: Eliminate Key Retirement Risks

Now that we know we can bridge the gap between monthly income and expenses with Guaranteed Lifetime Income, let's discuss how to remove the key retirement risks.

Sounds easy enough. How many retirement risks do you think there are? Four? Seven? The American College outlines 18 key risks to identify and eliminate when preparing to retire. I added one more to the list, and I will discuss all 19.

Like Tom Hegna, Curtis Cloke is another well-respected leader in the retirement space. He speaks to the country's financial leaders and consumers about retirement risks and methods to rewire retirement. Curtis may not be a household name, but he has a brilliant financial mind and is a key contributor to educating retirees and their advisors. In researching content for this book, I traveled to Madison, Wisconsin, to attend one of Cloke's symposiums, where he discussed much of the information included in this section.

Although this material can overwhelm readers, I encourage you to KEEP READING. Please do not quit now. You have come this far on your journey, and I promise not to bore you with risk classification and analysis.

Instead, let's play a game that I learned in college called "Three Truths and a Fib." I'm going to group these risks into four sections. At the end of each section, I'll share an embarrassing story about my first year in the business. Then, at the end of the book, after the "About the Author" section, I will reveal which statement is the fib! Anyway, let's dive into each of these risks and learn how you can neutralize each one.

Retirement Risks 1-5

1. Longevity Risk

Example: Longevity Risk is the risk that you will outlive your money. If you live past life expectancy and you continue to spend down your assets, you could potentially run out of money to maintain your standard of living.

How to Remove This Risk: Assess the present and future needs for monthly income, and then direct those needs to be paid with Guaranteed Lifetime Income. If your pension and Social Security do not meet those needs, the only optimal way to remove this risk is to use a Guaranteed Lifetime Income annuity.

Annuities must be laddered to turn passive cash flow on at varied phases to account for inflation or be indexed to inflation. This means that the payment aligns with the Consumer Price Index (CPI) and adjusts at the proper rate each year to account for the increased costs of goods and services. Typically, you can achieve a higher immediate income by laddering annuities.

Longevity is the most serious of all retirement risks because of its potential to increase the severity of other risks.

The longer you live, the higher the probability that you will face other or more serious risks.

2. Long-Term Care Risk

Example: Long-term care risk suggests you could become chronically ill or permanently disabled, requiring more of your income each month to pay expenses for care, which can be upwards of $150,000 per year.

Because costs for medical and long-term care are the greatest factors for bankruptcy in the US today, this is considered the second most significant retirement risk. Typically, this risk presents itself in the final years of life, quickly diminishing what you have left in your portfolio and forcing you to come up with $80,000 – $150,000 per year for an average of three or more years. Sadly, these figures are in today's numbers, and healthcare costs inflate by as much as seven percent per year. Imagine 30 years from now. This risk will have grown significantly higher.

If you have already planned for retirement and have not developed a way to remove this risk, your retirement voyage may be the Titanic. Without a plan or if you spend all your assets, you may qualify for state-provided care. For this reason, many people are afraid of the government and nursing homes taking all of their money because, in this scenario, you do not choose your quality of care. Guidelines vary from state to state, so please speak with an elder law attorney to discuss your situation. **This is not legal advice.**

How to Remove This Risk: Either self-insure or buy long-term care insurance. Because there are so many unknowns and the potential for increased costs in the future, most people remove this risk with insurance since it is easier to control with fixed premium costs. Retired millionaires self-insure. We can debate which way is better all day, but you buy insurance to remove risk. You can transfer any risk that would be detrimental to you to a large company built to absorb risk for a premium. You don't save money in case your house burns down. You buy a homeowner's insurance policy. You can do the same for retirement risk.

> **Note:** You can also purchase a special type of life insurance policy with a rider that will accelerate the policy's death benefit to you while you're alive if you qualify for one of the care-related claims specified in the policy.

3. Tax Risk

Example: Tax risk is the third most serious retirement risk and is becoming increasingly more dangerous. If you are on a fixed income generated from a fully taxable account, such as a 401(k), 403(b), IRA, TSA, TSP, SEP, SIMPLE, or a pension, and the government raises taxes, that can have a direct impact on your retirement. Tax Risk becomes far more worrisome.

In 2017, the Tax Reform Act was passed, which provided the lowest tax rates levied in the last 30 years. Considering the stimulus during the COVID-19 pandemic and our national debt, how likely do you think it is that the government will budget for a reduction in taxes again during your retirement? How likely is it that the government will need to raise taxes? If your income is fully taxable (it always will be) and taxes are increased by just 10 percent, you just realized a 10 percent loss of income forever.

Note: People often believe that you don't pay taxes on your retirement account savings or Social Security once you reach retirement. Both are false unless you only have taxable income in the zero percentage bracket and collect only your social security. **I am not a licensed CPA. Taxes may vary and are based on your individual situation. This is not tax advice.**

How to Remove This Risk: The only way to remove the tax risk is to diversify your taxes with Roth IRAs or potentially with Life Insurance. Both allow for tax-free withdrawals if you follow the stipulations provided by the IRS when using these structures. Having enough money in one of these two vehicles will give you the ability to control your tax bracket in retirement. If taxes go up, you can replace that income from one of the tax-free buckets.

4. Inflation Risk

Example: Inflation is the risk that costs of goods and services will continue to increase over time, creating a stealth tax on your money as your dollars will not buy as much as they used to. Prices of cars, homes, food and travel often increase over time, which can be challenging for someone on a fixed income.

How to Remove This Risk: There are three ways to remove the risk.

1. Cover all your needs with guaranteed lifetime income; then, you can hedge inflation by outpacing it with the returns on the rest of your money.

2. Use an annuity ladder that would trigger additional streams of higher-income banded over one to five years. In other words, every five years, you could turn on another income stream and have an increasing income forever.

3. Purchase annuities with inflation-indexed riders today that will automatically provide you with the cost of living adjustments (COLAs) annually, as Social Security does.

5. Excessive Withdrawal Risk

Example: This is the risk that you may withdraw too much money. As we discussed, the four percent rule is no longer considered a sustainable withdrawal rate. The potential problem with a two percent withdrawal rate is there is a much higher chance that you will need more than that. Taking too much money out too early in retirement can significantly decrease your chance of maintaining your standard of living.

How to Remove This Risk: Assign the withdrawal need to guaranteed lifetime income. You can guaranty 5-10 percent withdrawal rates from a portion of your money to cover these excessive withdrawals and decrease your chance of running out of money.

Hey, you made it! That wasn't too bad, right? We are 25 percent of the way there. It's time to play *Three Truths and a Fib*!

Three Truths and a Fib - Statement 1

As a new banker in a retail branch, I didn't consider the the potential of being robbed.

During my first day of training, I skipped the session on properly counting money to customers so I could attend another meeting on what to do in the event of a robbery.

When handing cash back to my first actual customer, I dropped it into their hand and told them how much it was without counting to them.

Retirement Risks 6-10

6. Sequence of Withdrawals Risk

Example: This risk relates to withdrawing too much of your money during downturns, creating a larger net loss and greater potential risks for the retiree. Once the money is withdrawn at a loss, it cannot rebound with the market, leading to larger withdrawals from your portfolio, thus accelerating your nest egg's spend down.

How to Remove This Risk: This risk can be removed in two ways.

1. Use a Guaranteed Lifetime Income annuity that will provide the same withdrawal for the rest of your life and does not change or require more money when there is a downturn.

2. Time Segmentation – The process in which you leave buckets of money in liquid safe vehicles such as a savings account or certain types of life insurance. Then, you will always have a bucket that isn't impacted by downturns, so you can control which bucket represents the optimal withdrawal choice.

7. Order of Returns Risk

Example: This risk arises when returns occur early in retirement, explaining why it's possible to average 10 percent returns, withdraw five percent, yet still run out of money. It doesn't seem possible at first glance. Still, suppose you average 10 percent a year in growth and lose money within the first two years of withdrawals. In that case, the probability of running out of money increases even if phenomenal returns follow.

How to Remove This Risk: The tactic for removing this risk is identical to *Sequence of Withdrawals Risk.*

1. Use a Guaranteed Lifetime Income annuity that will provide the same withdrawal for the rest of your life and does not change or require more money when there is a downturn.

2. Time Segmentation – The process in which you leave buckets of money in liquid safe vehicles such as a savings account or certain types of life insurance. Then, you will always have a bucket that isn't impacted by downturns, so you can control which bucket represents the optimal withdrawal choice.

8. Volatility Risk

Example: This risk occurs when market downturns siphon portions of the money needed for income and could cause you to run out of money.

How to Remove This Risk: Properly assess your risk capacity. For instance, if you need the money as an income source within the next five years and depend on receiving that income, it would not make sense to risk that money because you can't afford to lose it.

9. Interest Rate Risk

Example: Changing interest rates can negatively impact savings vehicles or loans set aside for interest, income, or capital for safe assets in retirement.

How to Remove This Risk The only way to remove this risk is to diversify from other assets or lending possibilities that are not directly tied to interest rates. As a good rule of thumb, if your savings are loaded too heavily in one category relative to your overall goals and needs, you could be taking on too much exposure to any of these risks.

10. Liquidity Risk

Example: This is the risk of not having enough liquidity to provide support if needed.

How to Remove This Risk: Maintain 12 months of liquid savings in a savings account earmarked for expenses. Some people use a line of credit or a home equity line of credit as a safety net. Some people don't budget, so it is difficult to determine what an appropriate reserve fund should look like. Review your bank statements for the last six months to determine the average of what you spend each month and then multiply it by 12.

Well, you're halfway through the risks.

Three Truths and a Fib - Statement 2

I was a new banker at one of the top producing branches in our region with several incredible banking and investment veterans. I was 22 years old, and this was my first job in finance.

One day, when I took my break in the lunchroom, our branch manager and top-performing business banker were having lunch as well. Still, on a tight post-college budget, I had purchased some ceviche from a discount grocer. That was my first mistake. When I opened the container, I immediately knew something was very wrong. A putrid smell filled the break room, causing my bank manager to exit immediately. My colleague also gathered up her things quickly and left as well.

Realizing that the fish must have turned sour, I walked over to the trash can and pitched it, deciding to pass on lunch and make my way back to my work station. Within 15 minutes, the smell migrated to the lobby. Soon, clients noticed. Quickly their faces displayed the expression one gets when a skunk is nearby.

Then, one of my coworkers yelled across the lobby, "Oh Danny, your disgusting lunch is stinking up the entire bank." She went to the break room and carried out the trash container holding my rotten fish as if she was carrying a bomb. I was so embarrassed. To this day, I have not ordered ceviche again.

11. Elder Abuse Risk

Example: This is, in my opinion, one of the most troubling risks relative to vulnerable seniors that happens when seniors are sold products or strategies that present far too much risk for their risk capacity. In some instances, it can result from fraud or theft with assets lost or stolen. Not only are advisors and fiduciaries are culprits of this abuse, but in some cases, family members drain the resources of their aging relative, leaving them destitute at the most vulnerable stage in their life.

How to Remove This Risk: There is no way to remove this risk entirely. Any senior not under constant supervision can suffer this abuse. However, safeguards, such as special documents and planning, can be put in place to help prevent financial elder abuse. For example, a trustworthy family member or a fiduciary is often assigned a durable power of attorney to manage the senior's finances. Trusts are another tool that may be employed with a trustee to oversee the assets for the senior.

A fiduciary is a person or organization that acts on behalf of another person or persons to manage assets with a responsibility by law to act in the person's best interests. Essentially, a fiduciary owes duties of good faith and trust to that other entity.

These safeguards can help protect a senior from giving away money, losing money or assets, or being sold a fraudulent product. All safeguards, however, are only as strong as the integrity of the person executing it. Specific laws make the trustee, power of attorney, and fiduciary legally liable should they violate their fiduciary obligation.

12. Employer Solvency Risk

Example: This risk occurs when an employer goes out of business, furloughs, or lays off employees just as they are ready to retire, and is becoming an increasingly more common risk. It can be very stressful working with clients in that final stretch leading up to their target retirement date, only to see them lose their job. Unfortunately, it happens. A person invests his time anticipating receiving employer retirement or other benefits only to be terminated before reaching their pension qualification period.

How to Remove This Risk: This risk can be removed by addressing two key factors. The first one may seem obvious, but it is essential to start preparing for retirement far sooner than the last few years of employment. Planning to retire on only earnings made in the last few years of employment involves too much risk.

Another tactic to alleviate this risk is to create other income streams to decrease the dependency on your wages. For instance, you can have a "side hustle" or gig or business that you run to produce another stream of income. Other options are real estate, annuities, and dividends — anything that produces income that can bridge employment gaps.

Addressing these key factors will give you more control and flexibility during the years leading up to retirement. They will certainly reduce stress and allow for a more peaceful entrance into retirement.

13. Reemployment Risk

Example: This risk occurs when a person plans to work in retirement, returning to the workforce as a part-time employee or in a different field. Often, circumstances change, preventing this plan from being realized. Declining health or issues with an employer can make this re-entrance difficult or even impossible.

How to Remove This Risk: Removing this risk can be challenging and may require preparation to branch out into a different form of employment. For example, if you planned on working in a department store, but you cannot find a job doing this, or your health or circumstances prevent you from applying for that job, you may need to research working from home or gain a new skill.

For instance, if you have excellent grammar and punctuation skills, you can work from home online as a proofreader. There are unique marketplaces and opportunities that will allow you to translate your skills into income using your phone or computer. These opportunities don't discriminate due to age or health, and many times may provide more compensation than traditional employment.

14. Forced Retirement Risk

Example: By now, you can tell that many of these risks are self-explanatory. This risk occurs when your employer or unexpected circumstances, such as failing health (yours or a family member's), forces you to retire earlier than expected.

How to Remove This Risk: Again, like Reemployment, you can remove this risk by not planning to solidify your retirement in the final stretch of your career. Remember, the shorter your timeline, the greater the risk.

This principle is not necessarily true relative to your human capital and is centered around your scope of retirement. When you are working, the younger you are and the more earning potential you have, the higher your earning capital. If you were to pass away at an early age, your family would not receive the earnings for all those years you could have potentially worked.

To protect your family from this risk, you may purchase term life insurance to replace the lost earning potential caused by your premature death. More on this topic when we cover mortality and economic spouse risk.

15. Frailty Risk

Example: Another risk that occurs as we age and our physical and mental faculties begin to fail is Frailty. When employees can no longer perform tasks needed to operate in the workplace, a forced retirement could impact the standard of living. Frailty risk also encompasses the need for long-term care.

How to Remove This Risk: This risk can be neutralized by purchasing disability insurance to pay lost wages. Retirement income should be built to provide enough money to enjoy your current standard of living and cover your basic needs and expenses. This income should be set to adjust to provide for additional expenses should healthcare costs increase with age.

You have completed 75 percent of the retirement risks. Hooray! Here's the next story.

Three Truths and a Fib - Statement 3

One day while I was helping a young teenager set up a checking account, his dad interrupted and asked if we had Private Banking at our branch. I responded, "Yes, we do. Let me get one for you. I'll be right back, buddy."

The man replied, "I am 30 years older than you, and I am NOT your buddy." Embarrassed, I hurried off to get the banker.

It turns out he was a wealthy businessman who ended up bringing his business to our bank. Although he made a point to be rude to me each time he came into the bank, I was given credit for bringing in the business and received a promotion soon after.

16. Mortality Risk

Example: This is the risk that you die too soon, either before retirement or in retirement. If others, such as spouses or children, depend on your support, and should you die early, they would struggle.

To mitigate this risk, first, evaluate your human capital— the monetary value your life represents in future payments to your household. For example, if you make $100,000 per year and plan to work 20 more years, but you unexpectedly die today, your family would lose $2,000,000. (There is a more accurate way to calculate your human capital, but this gives you a rough idea.)

If you receive a pension and choose a straight life-only option upon retirement, that pension would stop when you die, creating another mortality risk. This is particularly financially hard on the surviving spouse for two reasons. They will only receive the higher of the two Social Security checks, and their federal income tax filing status will move from joint to single, which is generally a more costly proposition. Once again, your human capital will need to be assessed and accounted for. Remember, the younger you are, the higher your human capital because of the added potential and time to earn more money.

How to Remove This Risk: Generally, you can remove this risk with life insurance, which allows you to assess your human capital and any other provisions if you pass away.

When you're young, term insurance is one of the most efficient ways to neutralize this risk. There is a heated debate about which type of life insurance policy is the best and how much coverage should be purchased.

LIMRA, a life insurance research organization, tells us that term policies pay out the death benefit for less than two percent of policyholders. How else could a 30-year-old write an $18 check, die in a car accident, and have a $1,000,000 claim paid to his or her family by the insurance company? That doesn't seem like a profitable business model. But 98 percent of the time, that does not happen.

Many people believe the group term life insurance policy included with their employee benefits package is sufficient. However, 70 percent of Americans are underinsured, meaning that their survivors would run out of money in less than two and a half years if that individual were to pass away.

I often hear, "Oh, I get coverage through work. I have five times my salary—$500,000." That seems like a lot of money, but add up the mortgage, the kids' college, weddings, charitable intentions, your spouse's retirement. That easily exceeds the $500K your employer life insurance offered you, plus you will no longer be contributing earnings to offset these costs. You can do the math and see how quickly your family would be left severely financially and emotionally harmed.

Is this the right thing for a retiree to do? What if they have enough assets? The risk may not be a threat to the family or surviving spouse's lifestyle. Retirees have to be extremely careful because of the misinformation that is common when discussing life insurance. We are taught to buy a 20-year term policy, build our net worth until the kids are grown, and the mortgage is paid off, and you won't need life insurance. For some people, that is true. For the majority of people, it is false. Buying term and investing the difference only works if you invest the difference, but the truth is, most people spend it.

When you retire, human capital transitions into what I have often heard referred to as *the economic impact of losing your spouse*. It is that scenario I discussed earlier where predeceasing your spouse could cut income down by as much as 70 percent. Put another way, when you're working, your human capital is how much you will earn each year until you retire. Once you retire, your income from pensions and Social Security will only continue as long as you are living. If you pass away, this will stop or reduce income to your household for your spouse or family.

Today, seniors are the greatest demographic purchasing life insurance.

In addition to life insurance, you could also choose annuity and pension income streams that provide joint-life payouts which cover both spouses as long as they live to help reduce the impact of mortality risk.

17. Unexpected Financial Responsibility Risk

Example: This risk occurs when you unexpectedly are required to assume financial responsibility for something or someone and are not prepared to do so. Typically, this is when you accept responsibility for an elderly parent or even your adult children who are forced to move back in with you due to lack of employment. Baby Boomers are now known as the sandwich generation because they often support both their parents and their adult children, creating a burden on retirement savings.

How to Remove This Risk: This risk is difficult to plan for or deal with because there are many variations. While there are strategies that can remove the financial responsibilities that these risks present, the best way to mitigate the risks is through healthy communication and boundaries. If you can be proactive and begin a good dialogue with your family, you can avoid many painful circumstances.

Some options to alleviate this may include combinations of funding long-term care policies or life insurance and paying housing costs for your aging parents. While you are still financially responsible, this option permits you to maintain your freedom and lifestyle.

A parent who is facing financial difficulties and moves in with their adult child can offer part of their Social Security check to help defer the added costs of living there. Discussing finances with your loved ones early could be the difference between helping them before it is too late and picking up the pieces.

18. Timing Risk

Example: This risk occurs frequently. When you buy or sell an investment at the wrong time, causing you to miss out on a better return or lose money, it's a timing risk. For instance, instead of investing a large sum of money into the market, add smaller amounts periodically to avoid buying high and selling low.

How to Remove This Risk: As experts like Warren Buffett have stated repeatedly, "You cannot time the market." Dollar-cost averaging and consistently purchasing will allow you to capture seasonality. Sometimes you will buy assets at a higher price, and other times, at a discount. Our market history shows that you eliminate timing risk and consistently profit when you hold assets and consistently buy.

Once again, this is not investment advice. Also, it is important to know that buy and hold has always worked. Remember, though, as I said earlier, *buy and hold* no longer works in retirement. Instead, it's *hold and distribute*. This means that timing, order of returns, and sequence of withdrawals risks all come back into play. If the market crashes and you must sell to make a withdrawal, you will feel the negative impact of these risks, and longevity risk comes back into play. The longer you live, the more you must withdraw. Plus, the more you're exposed to timing risk, the greater the probability that you'll run out of money. Assigning the amount of income you'll need to an annuity will remove all these risks. Then, you can dollar cost average with the rest of your money to avoid timing risk.

19. Public Policy Risk

Example: This is the risk that laws could change, impacting your retirement. Two recent examples of this were the Bipartisan Budget ACT of 2015 and the SECURE ACT of 2019.

The Bipartisan Budget Act of 2015 swiftly removed the restricted application for future Social Security recipients. When this happened, it ripped billions of dollars out of the hands of future retirees who had worked and earned that money.

The Secure Act of 2019 changes the provisions on inheriting qualified plans from non-spouses. Beneficiaries must now distribute those assets within ten years instead of spreading the distribution out over their lifetime. This subtle change can potentially increase tax brackets, substantially reducing an inheritance.

How to Remove This Risk: There really is no way to mitigate or remove this risk. However, there are historical precedents that you can observe, which may decrease the probability of impacting your retirement if this risk occurs.

One notable observation is that the government has always allowed a grandfather provision. For instance, the government has never voided the tax-free privileges for individuals who have existing Roth IRA and life insurance accounts if new laws are enacted. Instead, changes that eliminate benefits will apply only to new accounts or policies.

It's best not to delay using these tools while they are available. You can set up an account with minimal funds now and revisit that strategy later should you need it.

Three Truths and a Fib - Statement No. 4

I almost missed my first day of training for the JP Morgan investment licenses program. I was stuck in South Carolina during a hurricane. Most flights were canceled. I couldn't get a flight to Phoenix but could get the last seat on a flight to Los Angeles. I caught a red-eye from LA to Phoenix and made it to my first day of investment training just in time. The rest is history!

So, do you think you know which story is the fib? Remember to check for the answer after the *About the Author* section.

Conclusion

Many retirement risks can be neutralized in one of two ways:

1. Grow your net worth, so it is greater than the sum of the quantified risk.

2. Transfer the risk to an insurance company that will guarantee to eliminate the risk for a premium.

Example: If future long-term healthcare costs are projected to be $560,000 (with inflation factored in) for a 65-year-old couple retiring today, as long as they have more than $560,000 in liquid net worth (not their home or other non-liquid assets), then the risk is not a threat.

If they do not have that amount of money, they can take a portion of their liquid net worth and trade it for a guaranteed insurance policy that will provide the funds for care when needed, protecting their other assets.

Remember, insurance has its place even when you have assets. Sometimes, a retirement specialist worth their title will calculate if an insurance policy will benefit a couple by shielding their assets and allowing them time to perform, or if it is wiser to use the insurance company's money instead of their own.

An annuity is often the most efficient way to transfer these risks to a company built to deal with these expenses. This method is neither pro- nor anti-annuity. Annuities probably have the most significant stigma of any of these financial products—right up there with the reverse mortgage. However, in the white paper **"Retirement Alpha,"** we find the proof and scientific research pointing to annuities as the optimal choice to fulfill the need for income on top of social security and pensions in retirement.

It's like you need to cross the Grand Canyon on an old rickety wooden bridge that is missing floorboards, and the annuity represents guaranteed safe passage all the way across. It is certainly not the only available tool, but it does its job.

Retirement is not about building wealth for most people. Most people build their wealth before retirement to provide income, so they no longer have to work. Transferring portions of net worth to annuities provides guaranteed passive income for life, regardless of economic conditions.

The difference between the accumulation phase of building your wealth and the decumulating phase can be compared to a farmer planting and harvesting the crops. Too many consumers and planners are stuck in the growth-only mindset. They do not see the benefits of treating each phase according to its purpose. They see growth as the only tool to fulfill such goals as income distributions and mitigate risks such as inflation, long-term care expenses, and taxes.

Consider our farmer comparison. It would be like the farmer trying to grow many, many more crops than is sustainable. Relying on growth could work, and it may ultimately provide more money to your heirs, but it also could fail, forcing your heirs to support you.

Your choices depend on your unique circumstances and goals. If you have a net worth of $10,000,000, no debt, you only need $24,000 in additional income annually after Social Security, and you have an average lifespan with no pressing health concerns, then, yes, I see the goal of building your net worth.

However, if you have not taken these key retirement risks off the table and you're gambling with money you cannot afford to lose, this signals the need to transfer those risks. Insurance companies play a crucial role in retirement for these very reasons. Their business is to remove risks for you, literally ensuring the success of your retirement and providing you with peace of mind.

Key Takeaways

- You can establish the most optimal retirement strategy by employing this Two-Step process. These philosophies were brought into the mainstream by the economist

Tom Hegna, the retirement authority in the United States.

- Tom's work in this space results from the dedicated study of hundreds of white papers from PhDs, physicists, and economists.

- These professionals unanimously agree that longevity risk is the most significant risk to retirees because of increasing life expectancies.

- The only way to optimally retire is by establishing Guaranteed Lifetime Income and removing the risks that threaten that income.

Bonuses

The Two-Step process outlined in this book is practiced by most major financial firms in the United States, thanks to these economists. However, some strategies differentiate and can make a meaningful impact on your retirement. While the methods above are considered conventional, the following bonus strategies can expedite your retirement's success.

The bonus concepts described below have made the most significant impact in the lives of Americans, allowing them to achieve financial freedom and retire early, so these must be shared.

Topics include:

Social Security Maximization

Eighty percent of Americans take their Social Security to their detriment. Get 32 percent more benefits and the highest income possible while maximizing your benefits using Professor Laurence Kotlikoff's formula. He is the foremost authority on Social Security in the United States and is among the world's top 25 most influential economists.

Watch a video explanation here:

retirementsimplified.org/ssmax

Pension Maximization

Take the higher income and guarantee you can pass all of your pension payments to your spouse in a lump sum, tax-free after you have passed.

Watch a video explanation here:

retirementsimplified.org/penmax

Tax-Free Withdrawal Privilege

Three ways to get taxable income out of your fully-taxable accounts without paying any taxes.

Watch a video explanation here:

retirementsimplified.org/taxfree

Pay Off Your 30-Year Fixed Mortgage in Five Years

Yes, you read that right. There is a strategy to do this without increasing your income. It depends on your goal, but it is possible! I practice it personally, as I do with many of these bonuses.

Some people read this and think, "Why would I do this when interest rates are so low?" Well, the simple answer is, it depends on your goals. I am not writing this to convince you that this is a good idea. I am presenting another way to pay off your house even if it is financed at a low interest rate.

If your financial advisor tried to convince you to borrow money against your home at these low rates to invest in the stock market, would you do it? No, and you'd probably fire them. Keeping a mortgage because the rates are low so you can invest in the same exact thing. Now think about it from the bank's perspective. A bank will charge you 3% on the most significant amount of money you'll most likely ever borrow but pay you virtually nothing on the most amount of money you can save after taxes to put into your savings account? Do you think the bank would rather have an investment that requires you to pay them steady cash flow on a secured asset for 30 years or for you to own your home free and clear?

Think about it from the mortgage broker's perspective. They love when interest rates go down, and they help you refinance. A mortgage is front-loaded with fees and interest, so they will collect those fees again. There is nothing wrong with these professions. We are a culture that is addicted to the 30-year fixed mortgage. It's safe and cozy, but it's our largest monthly bill for most of us and blocks the way to financial freedom. So again, it depends on your goal, but it is possible!

Watch a video explanation here:

retirementsimplified.org/nomortage

Time Horizon

How to assess your runway to retirement to make sure that you are appropriately adjusting your needs to prepare for retirement.

Watch a video explanation here:

retirementsimplified.org/assessment

Medicare Mastery

How to make sure that you have the right coverage and don't spend a lifetime overpaying for the wrong supplement insurance.

Watch a video explanation here:

retirementsimplified.org/medicare

Risk Capacity

A risk analysis will determine how susceptible you are to these key retirement risks.

Watch a video explanation here:
retirementsimplified.org/assessment

Goals

How to clearly outline and define your goals and remove any unnecessary distractions that will deter you from reaching them.

Watch a video explanation here:
retirementsimplified.org/assessment

Travel Hacking

How to earn free travel and take a vacation every year by leveraging airline reward points.

Watch a video explanation here:
retirementsimplified.org/travelhacking

Stopping Your Mortgage Payments and Protecting Your Equity

This is the fastest way to provide the highest cash flow and give you instant tax-free access to money, neutralizing some of the key retirement risks without requiring any investment.

Watch a video explanation here:

retirementsimplified.org/stopmypayment

Add Long-Term Care and Life Insurance Benefits Without Paying Any Premiums

Add these benefits to your savings, annuities, and IRAs at no cost.

Watch a video explanation here:

retirementsimplified.org/ltcbenefits

Inheritance, Estate, Legacy

Schedule a complimentary consultation with an estate planning attorney who can evaluate your estate plan and help facilitate the proper supporting documentation to protect you.

Watch a video explanation here:

retirementsimplified.org/legacy

College Planning

Guarantee the highest amount of tax-free money for your college savings without disqualifying your future students from qualifying for FAFSA and government loan and grant programs.

Watch a video explanation here:
retirementsimplified.org/collegeplan

Complete a Balance Sheet and Income Statement

These are two of the most important financial documents that will allow you to precisely identify how your financial situation operates.

Watch a video explanation here:
retirementsimplified.org/assessment

Digital Assets

Digital Assets will be one of the most relevant ways to earn income in retirement over the next ten years. Digital arbitrage, which sounds intimidating, is quite simple and almost magical for a retiree. It has never been easier to earn a meaningful income from home with your phone and your time. Think about someone who retired and does not have enough money. What are they supposed to do?

Well, digital assets can be created with time instead of cash. For instance, you can start a YouTube channel with your phone and zero dollars and monetize it to be a meaningful revenue source. Every day, bloggers, influencers, coaches, and others create online courses, eBooks, videos, and podcasts to create real income.

Retirees are the perfect people to master these tools and arbitrage all of their time and knowledge into a digital marketplace that will pay them very well for their value. Someone living on $32,000 per year from Social Security benefits could earn another $750 a month—$9,000 a year. That would be a 28% increase in their retirement income. Many retirees have the time to invest to increase it even more. Digital assets and digital real estate you own in the marketplaces to earn income today will someday be like buying dirt on the Las Vegas Strip in the 1920s.

Watch a video explanation here:

retirementsimplified.org/digitalassets

For access to a free tutorial on implementing these strategies and a personalized complimentary evaluation of your situation, visit:

www.DanielRondberg.com

Here, you can book a private one-on-one call with a member of my national team of professionals. My team currently oversees $100 million in retirement assets and has helped more than 10,000 people retire successfully.

About The Author

Daniel Rondberg

The Retirement Specialist

Daniel Rondberg is a retirement authority that has been featured multiple times in different publications like Yahoo Finance, Forbes, Bloomberg, and USA Today. He is an international best-selling author with a huge mission: to reach as many people as possible with powerful easy to read, and apply financial non-fiction books to help them achieve what they want out of life!

Daniel lives in Gilbert, Arizona, together with her lovely wife, Jennifer, and daughters Cassidy and Spencer, with whom he plays castles and princesses every Sunday.

Before he started writing financial strategy books, Danny began working as a banker for JP Morgan Chase until he eventually shifted his focus as an independent retirement specialist and joined his father's company, educating people on tax reduction methods and retirement security. However, his greatest strength is listening closely to his clients and alleviating their concerns by providing customized solutions that align with their core beliefs. Daniel has since left his father's company to expand his reach after nine years of working to help people with traditional retirement methods. He desires to combine his conventional retirement application strategies with his new innovative ideas about creating income with new tools and technology to improve our quality of life.

He teaches educational workshops on traditional and new retirement methods to both financial professionals and consumers. He is a contributor as an author for one of the leading experts on retirement, Tom Hegna. He has co-authored books such as *Digital Retirement* and *Letters To Our Younger Selves* with Michelle Kulp .

He has gone on to become an international bestselling author with his books:

1) **No Stone Left Unturned: How to Cash In On This Hidden Treasure in the Tax Code**
   https://www.amazon.com/dp/1734961309/

2) **Retirement Simplified: The Simple Two-Step Formula to Retire Wealthy & Worry-Free**
   https://www.amazon.com/dp/1734961333/

Featured Book!

3) **Pay Off Your Mortgage: Pay Down Your Biggest Debt Fast, The Key to Financial Freedom**
   https://www.amazon.com/dp/1734961317/

4) **Retirement Through Passive Income: How to Retire Early and Create Meaningful Income**

https://www.amazon.com/dp/1734961325

Danny is known to many for his dedication in helping people to achieve retirement. Whatever you define that as. If you would like to speak with a financial professional on Daniel's team, please call (602) 671-0797.

Connect with Daniel Rondberg

My Personal Site: https://www.danielrondberg.com
My Vlog: https://www.retirementbydanielrondberg.com
My YouTube Channel:
https://www.youtube.com/channel/UCkdozAYowONtAeyNaU30hfg
My Podcast: http://www.buzzsprout.com/695890
My Facebook: https://www.facebook.com/danielrondberg58
My LinkedIn: https://www.linkedin.com/in/daniel-rondberg-99686572

Answer to Three Truths and a Fib

Sadly, these are all true. I really was a knucklehead when I joined the financial industry. Thankfully I had many great mentors and clients who believed in me and whipped me into shape.

Sources

www.forbes.com/sites/andrewbiggs/2016/09/20/how-many-americans-are-saving-for-retirement-how-many-should-be/#707b7b946705

"Don't Worry, Retire Happy" – Tom Hegna

"Retirement Alpha" – Tom Hegna

https://internet.beethoven.de/en/exhibition/beethovens-capital/id2.htmln

business.time.com/2012/05/04/why-annuities-are-the-answer-but-such-a-tough-sell/

www.protectedincome.org/annuities/retirement-happiness-studies-article/

https://www.investopedia.com/terms/s/

"Danger Zone" - Curtis Cloke

www.protectedincome.org/annuities/retirement-happiness-studies-article/

Retirement Simplified is the summary of my interpretation of Tom Hegna's body of work, specifically, but not limited to, "Pay Checks and Play Checks," "Don't Worry, Retire Happy,"

"Retirement Alpha," and his collection of video and audio content.

Made in the USA
Monee, IL
28 July 2021